MW01415188

IF FOUND PLEASE RETURN TO:

THIS SECOND HALF CHRONICLES
JOURNAL OWNER WILL GIVE YOU
THE MOST VALUABLE ADVICE
IF YOU'LL STOP AND HAVE A LISTEN!

MY
Second Half

CHRONICLES JOURNAL

IT'S YOUR SECOND HALF, LIVE IT BOLDLY

HANDS DOWN IN MY SECOND HALF I WILL....

MY
Second Half

CHRONICLES JOURNAL

Fulfilling dreams, thriving,
and living boldly in My Second Half!

Created by:
Cavami Olsen

IT'S YOUR SECOND HALF, LIVE IT BOLDLY

HANDS DOWN IN MY SECOND HALF I WILL...

Copyright © 2024 Carami Olsen.

All rights reserved. No part of this document may be reproduced or transmitted in any form or by any means, electronic, mechanical, photocopying, recording, or otherwise, without prior written permission of Carami Olsen.

Published by Second Half, LLC
ISBN: 979-8-9898734-0-1

The content within this interactive journal is intended to stimulate critical thinking, promote reflective learning, and encourage intellectual engagement. While every effort has been made to ensure the accuracy and completeness of the content, the publisher makes no representations or warranties, either express or implied, regarding the reliability, suitability, or availability of the information presented. Any reliance you place on the information within this interactive journal is at your own risk. The publisher, editors, and authors shall not be held liable for any errors, omissions, or inaccuracies in the content or for any actions taken in reliance thereon. Readers are encouraged to independently verify information and seek professional advice when necessary.

~ CONNECT ~
secondhalfchronicles.com
@secondhalfchronicles
secondhalfchronicle@gmail.com

Dedication

To those who might have lost a little of themselves along the road of life...which is all of us.
To those who want to discover what how it feels as you fulfill dreams, experience passions, and target goals as you approach, shift, or thrive in the Second Half of your life!

table of contents

What to Expect

Why Second Half?

What's Your Definition?

Self Reflection Quiz

Skills Acquired in My First Half

Dreams that Got Away

Vision Board

One Year Plan

Five Year Plan

Ten Year Plan

Twenty Year Plan

Journal Prompts

Journal Pages

My Adieu

Those of us in our Second Half, this is where the most fun really happens.
We aren't bound by the expectations of what other people think.

April Little
Stylist & Coach

What to Expect

Remember that All About Me project you did in 1st grade? Well this journal is kind of like that, but revealing yourself now, as a mature (maybe), experienced (YES), wise (YES), and more skilled version of that first grader. Plan on exploring: What do I actually like? What do I not like? How am I willing to spend my time...because that's what I'm doing...is spending, spending, spending. This journal will reinforce this idea:

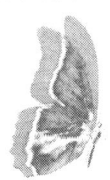

> I am privileged to be in the Second Half of my life and time is precious.
> How am I going to spend it?

This book's exercises are designed to garner an active mindset for pivoting into or optimizing your Second Half days. Move through the exercises at your own pace and in which ever order you feel inclined. Use the prompts to spawn focused journal entries and *journal any time between exercises!* Most of all:

Enjoy the journey of chronicling your Second Half!

Why Second Half?

None of us know when it's our turn to go. My sisters and I have always claimed that we will outlive everyone in our family, especially the men. A boastful claim? Maybe. Derived from facts? We think so.

As I approached my 47th birthday I pondered the abundant lives which both of my grandmothers lived throughout each of their 94 years. Reflecting on these women's journeys caused me to think: if both of my grandmothers lived through life's challenges with poise, integrity and grit until age 94, then I very well could do the same! Quick mental math of their passing age revealed that I could possibly have a complete half to go!

That realization lit me on fire!! I started to feel unmistakably alive again. My visionary spirit arose out and beyond the dregs of day to day survival where it had been squirreled away for so many years. Familiar childhood feelings sprang up: curiosity and hopefulness. I felt almost reborn and deeply inquisitive about all the things my future days had to offer. Strolling into my 48th trip around the sun I figured that I must live as though I have another 47 exquisite years to do what I need to do here! I believe that particular awareness gave me a renewed energy, a fresh hope, and a peek into a splendid unfolding horizon.

♡ *Cavarni*

What's Your Definition?

Second Half begins at a different age and is a unique experience for everyone. Many have an awakening which defines or deems their Second Half beginning. "They" might call this a midlife crisis, but we are throwing that term in the toilet. We are putting a positive spin on this glorious pivot.

Some endure a traumatic experience which is more than any human should be required to sustain. Emerging on the other side of that usually marks the beginning of a Second Half - no matter the age. We have all been through difficult changes, trials and slump times. We've all had days and moments that we have wanted to crawl into bed and put our head under the covers forever. That is what makes this Second Half notion so beautiful. We can take all that we've learned from those undesirable situations and use that to our advantage in our future. In our Second Half, we can open back up and allow our creative and inventive side to come out of hibernation. Where it will take us over the next decades?

Of course we really don't know when it's our time to go, and some leave this earth many years sooner than any of us feel is fair. We cannot predict the future from disease and accidents...but we can't hide out and be scared. When we have the privilege of living longer, can we please give ourselves the forward-looking perspective that life does not end in our 40's? That idea needs to be squashed! We still have lots of havoc to wreak! Be confident that you have something important to live for in your Second Half! What's the harm in celebrating the Second Half - whatever your definition may be? Now it's your turn to define it.

Describe the defining moment your Second Half began:

_____

_____

_____

_____

Free yourself from the stuckness from your past so that you can live in the now and move forward

Yoggi Parmar
Home Organization Coach

Self Reflection Quiz

1 **What skill have you acquired over the years that you are most proud of?**

a Mastering a new language
b Leadership and team-building
c Advanced technical or digital skills
d Expertise in a creative field like writing, painting, or music
e Proficiency in working with your hands or tools

2 **When you think about your dreams, which one excites you the most?**

a Traveling to new and exotic destinations
b Starting your own business
c Pursuing further education or learning a new subject
d Launching a passion project that combines creativity and purpose
e Engaging in hands-on, creative endeavors or craftsmanship

3 **What role do your friendships play in your life now?**

a They are a source of joy and shared experiences
b Networking and professional connections are crucial
c A mix of both personal and professional connections
d Supportive allies who encourage your creative pursuits
e Valuable relationships that involve collaborative, hands-on activities

4. Which statement best reflects your attitude towards change and adaptation?

a. Chang is inevitable; I embrace it wih an open mind
b. I thrive in dynamic environments and seek new challenges
c. Change can be challenging, but it presents opportunities for growth
d. I believe in adapting to change while staying true to my values
e. I am open to adapting through hands-on solutions and practical skills

5. What motivates you to set new goals for yourself?

a. The desire for personal fulfillment and happiness
b. The opportunity to make a positive impact on others
c. A combination of personal and professional success
d. The chance to express your unique creativity and talents
e. The satisfaction of achieving tangible, hands-on accomplishments

6. If you were to attend a workshop or class, what topic would you be most excited to explore?

a. Mindfulness and well-being
b. Entrepreneurship and business strategy
c. Cutting-edge technology and innovation
d. Expressive arts and creative writing
e. Hands-on skills or craftsmanship in a specific field

7. How do you envision your ideal work-life balance in this next phase of life?

a. Prioritizing self-care and enjoying leisure activites
b. Pursuing a fulfilling career while maintaining personal connections
c. Balancing work, personal growth, and meaningful relationships
d. Integrating creativity and passion into daily life
e. Incorporating hands-on activities into your routine

8. What do you believe is the key to maintaining a positive mindset during transitions?

- a Cultivating gratitude and focusing on the present moment
- b Setting clear goals and taking decisive action
- c Seeking support from friends, mentors, and loved ones
- d Expressing yourself through creative outlets and self-reflection
- e Approaching challenges with a hands-on problem-solving mindset

9. Which statement resonates with your approach to taking risks at this stage in your life?

- a I'm open to calculated risks that align with my values
- b I see challenges as opportunities for growth and innovation
- c I weigh the pros and cons before taking measured risks
- d I believe in taking creative risks that bring joy and fulfillment
- e I embrace risks that involve hands-on learning and skill building

10. When envisioning your legacy, what would you like to be remembered for?

- a Inspiring others to live authentically and joyfully
- b Making a significant impact in your professional field
- c Balancing success with kindness and positive relationships
- d Leaving a creative and artistic imprint on the world
- e Leaving a tangible impact through hands-on contributions

▶ Tally the occurrences of the letters. The letter with the highest count corresponds to the category that aligns most with your current mindset and aspirations.

Notes

What have you learned in your first half that can really launch your Second Half endeavors?

Skills acquired in my first half to propel me into a creative and fulfilling Second Half:

Take a moment to reflect on the skills and talents that make you exceptional. What are your abilities that set you apart? If you are in your Second Half, then you can definitely generate a long list of skills your mind and body have acquired. What do people compliment you on? Go crazy! List them here and pay attention to the ones you enjoy spending time doing or crave to do better:

skills~qualifications~abilities~credentials~talents

Dreams that got away...

Take a moment to transport yourself back to those days filled with limitless imagination and boundless possibilities. Go ahead and tap into your inner child! What were those whimsical aspirations that used to spark your imagination? Whether it was becoming an astronaut, a superhero, or a world traveler, each dream is a testament to the creativity and curiosity that defined your younger self.

Maybe your dreams dissipated as you transitioned into adulthood and had to start paying bills. Maybe you had to choose one aspiration over another, an opportunity cost, which cost you an entire childhood dream!

Or you gave up your own ambition to help someone else fulfill theirs. Revisit them now! Consider the joy and excitement you used to feel when dreaming about the future. Remember, dreams are not confined to the past - they evolve and transform over time. You can think of at least 10 dreams you had as a youth or young adult when the world didn't hinder you from imagining a life of possibility.

Writing these down will allow you to rediscover forgotten passions, uncover hidden talents, and find new ways to incorporate elements of those dreams into your Second Half!

Detail dreams, desires, and hopes that you had in your youth.

_____

_____

_____

_____

_____

_____

VISION ~ REALITY

DREAMS ~ ASPIRATIONS

Create a word vision board that represents your manifestations for the next chapter of your Second Half.

GOALS ~ MOTIVATION

PLACES ~ EXPERIENCES

IT'S YOUR SECOND HALF, LIVE IT BOLDLY

HANDS DOWN IN MY SECOND HALF I WILL....

My Vision Board

When you realize the possibility of living another entire Second Half of life, you start to feel curious again, like a child. Learning is delicious.

Carami Olsen
Author & Creator

One Year Plan

IT'S YOUR SECOND HALF, LIVE IT BOLDLY

HANDS DOWN IN MY SECOND HALF I WILL...

This is my ME era

April Little
Stylist & Coach

Five Year Plan

IT'S YOUR SECOND HALF, LIVE IT BOLDLY

HANDS DOWN IN MY SECOND HALF I WILL....

The world needs to realize that those in their Second Half are...maybe just getting their first wind.

Michelle Ould
Advanced Aesthetician

Ten Year Plan

IT'S YOUR SECOND HALF, LIVE IT BOLDLY

HANDS DOWN IN MY SECOND HALF I WILL...

The world needs to realize that those in their Second Half are...funnier, richer, prettier, viable, we have wisdom and more patience hopefully.

Erin Pierson Mills
Influencer & Realtor

Twenty Year Plan

IT'S YOUR SECOND HALF, LIVE IT BOLDLY

HANDS DOWN IN MY SECOND HALF I WILL....

Journal Writing Prompts

Begin writing in the journal pages at any time throughout the process of these exploratory activities. Choose a prompt that resonates with your mood/vibe. They have been created to inspire and ignite energizing thoughts. Consider writing the journal prompt at the top of the page with the date. When you look back on your writing you will remember why you shared that scenario and situation. Go for it and **Chronicle your Second Half!!**

1. Do you feel like you've started living the Second Half of your life?

2. Describe one specific thing you will do in you Second Half that you haven't done in you first half.

3. If you had an open day with no obligations or any responsibilities, describe how you would spend your time.

4. Describe how you will remove yourself from your typical environment (physical/mental/emotional space) so you can get into a healthy mindset to go where you want to go and do what you want to do.

5. What's your next move?

6. Reflect: How did it go today? How did it go yesterday or this past week?

7. I learned something new...

8. I learned some new slang and use it...

9. I started something...

10. I revisited something that has been dormant for a while...

11. I finished something...YAY!!

12. I decluttered _____ and I feel so free!!

13. I booked that trip!!

14. I went on that trip!!

15. My fit was super sexy today, I'm just sayin'...

16. I scheduled that massage/treatment/spa day...

17. I volunteered today...

18. I had a meaningful conversation with someone quite a bit younger/older than me.

19. I respectfully explored and listened to another's perspective...

20. I shared/taught a skill to another.

21. I started a new project which will take time and resources. This is how it's going...

22. I can definitely say I overcame this challenge...

23. I felt really confident because...

24. I passed this valuable lesson on today...

25. I invited and met up with an old friend...

26. I am proud of my self today because...

Enjoy the journey of chronicling your Second Half!

My Adieu

The world needs to realize that those in their Second Half are...

I'd like to tell everyone in their first half to...

Hands down in my Second Half I will...

The world needs to realize that those in their Second Half are...

I'd like to tell everyone in their first half to...

Hands down in my Second Half I will...